To LaKeisha, Eleazar & Uriah

One Day at a Time: A Journey Through the Book of Proverbs
Published by Watersprings Media House, LLC.
P.O. Box 1284
Olive Branch, MS 38654
Contact publisher for permission requests and bulk orders.
www.waterspringsmedia.com

Copyright © 2018 Toussaint Williams. All rights reserved.

No portion of this book may be reproduced, stored in a retrieval system or transmitted in any form or by any means (electronic, mechanical, photocopy, recording, scanning, or other), except for brief quotations in critical reviews of articles, without the prior written permission of the writer.

Unless otherwise noted, Bible texts in this book are from the King James Version. Scripture quotations credited to NASB are from the New American Standard Bible, copyright © 1960, 1962, 1963, 1968, 1971, 1972, 1973, 1975, by the Lockman Foundation. Used by permission.

Scripture quotations credited to NIV are from the Holy Bible, New International Version. Copyright © 1973, 1978, 1984, 2011 by Biblica, Inc. Used by permission. All rights reserved worldwide.
Scripture quotations from THE MESSAGE, Copyright © by Eugene H. Peterson 1993, 1994, 1995, 1996, 2000, 2001, 2002. Used by permission of NavPress Publishing Group.

Scripture quotations marked "NKJV" are taken from the New King James Version. Copyright © 1982 by Thomas Nelson, Inc. Used by permission. All rights reserved.

Printed in the United States of America.

Library of Congress Control Number: 2018960074
ISBN 13: 978-1-948877-03-9
ISBN 10: 1-948877-03-1

One Day at a Time

A Journey Through the Book of Proverbs

31- Day Devotional

by

Toussaint Williams

Watersprings
PUBLISHING

Table of Contents

Introduction 6

Day 1: Own It! 9

Day 2: He Still Speaks 13

Day 3: Embrace The Pain! 16

Day 4: Obedience = Life 19

Day 5: Stay Faithful 22

Day 6: Find An Ant! 26

Day 7: Listen! 29

Day 8: Use Only Godly Words! 32

Day 9: Fear The Lord? 35

Day 10: Work Hard! 39

Day 11: Precious Things For Precious People 43

Day 12: You're Not That Smart! 46

Day 13: Discipline Won't Kill You! 49

Day 14: Tell The Truth 52

Day 15: Respond Kindly 55

Day 16: Let Him Lead! 58

Day 17: Stuff Or Satisfaction? 61

Day 18: Favor! 64

Day 19: Listen To Wise Counsel 67

Day 20: Work! 70

Table of Contents

Day 21: Help Somebody 74

Day 22: Focus On What Matters 77

Day 23: The Chase 80

Day 24: Man Up! 84

Day 25: Enough Is Enough 88

Day 26: Learn From Your Mistakes 91

Day 27: No Boasting! 95

Day 28: Be Bold! 99

Day 29: Walk Away 102

Day 30: Trust God 105

Day 31: Affirm Your Mom 108

Conclusion 112

About the Author 114

Introduction

If you are anything like me, you woke up this morning and rushed out of bed. Later, at some point during the day, after having something go crazy, you realized you neglected to spend time with God. Or maybe you wanted to spend time with Him but didn't know where to begin. For those who are wondering, "What do I need to focus on today?" The book of Proverbs has your answer!

During this month-long journey, we will focus on a specific verse from each chapter in Proverbs. The goal of this exercise is not for you to memorize the entire Bible or to master every concept of Biblical exegesis (i.e., a big word for in-depth Bible study), but simply to provide you with a very practical way to make your time with God meaningful, relevant, and consistent. Please don't read this book and assume it is for someone else or think that this process can be implemented another day. God has led you to this book to guide you--not for tomorrow or for a day in the distant future--but for TODAY!

Over the next 31 days, we are going to walk through the book of Proverbs. *One Day at a Time* is unique because it is *not* designed for you to rely on my words for study, nor are you to regurgitate my thoughts or become shackled to my way of thinking. This is a book to help **you** create habits for successful living! It is a personal challenge for you to identify how God is speaking to you for that specific day.

Throughout the book, I will cite the verse that spoke to me, then you will go back and read the chapter for that day. This 15-minute exercise will cause you to ask God, "Is there anything I need to apply to my life today?" Hopefully, you will become aware that the verse or thought that jumps out at you, the one that tugs at your heartstrings or irritates you to the point that it rings in your head after you put the Bible down, is probably the one that God wants you to focus on for that day. Space is provided for you to journal your thoughts about each text.

Remember, what you need today may be different next month. You can come back to this book again and again because your situation or focus might change. God may want to speak to you regarding another facet of your life, and when He does, LISTEN! The Christian journey is not easy, and you'll never have a dull moment, but the key is to trust God and watch Him carry you...*One Day at a Time!*

DAY ONE

꙰

Proverbs 1:1 (NIV)

The proverbs of Solomon the son of David, king of Israel.

꙰

Own It!

How does the wisest man on earth start his thoughts on life? Does he begin with his wealth? The keys to success? The time where he heard the voice of God in the temple? No, Solomon starts by telling the reader who he is! He owns his work by boldly connecting himself with a man many would be ashamed to call dad.

Solomon, he begins with the ugly truth! He immediately proclaims his lineage: "the son of David, king of Israel!" It is a simple statement yet has such profound implications. You remember David, right? He had an adulterous affair with Bathsheba while her husband, Uriah, was serving at war. During their rendezvous a child was conceived so David devised a scheme to cover up his actions. Because his "clever" plot was unsuccessful, David proceeded to orchestrate Uriah's death. Sadly, that innocent baby paid the ultimate price for his parents' sins yet opened the way for Solomon to become king.

God chose David while in the fields as a shepherd boy. Yet, the success of his kingship and the blessings of God must have led David to believe that he was invincible. His acts, if committed today, would earn him life in prison! However, David repented of his wrongdoings (see Psalm 51) and God in His mercy, allowed David to remain king. Not only that, his son, Solomon, inherited a throne filled with great peace as a result of David's loving relationship with God.

Today, just as you are standing, or sitting, or listening on iTunes, honor those that will come after you by repenting of your wrongdoing. Right now, simply say, "God I did _____ and I'm sorry. Please forgive me!" David said, "God I did it! I was wrong, and I acknowledge my transgressions. Father, please heal and restore me! When you finish chastising me Lord, please help me to teach others so they won't make the same mistake!" As an outgrowth of his prayer, God blessed Solomon and made him the wisest and most successful king in Israelite history.

As you begin this daily journey, it would be appropriate to acknowledge where you are in your relationship with Him. Own up to it! Then, ask Him to forgive you! Not only will He forgive you, but He will also bless you *and* your descendants long after you're gone. Spend time with the Lord today and watch how He transforms your life and those you love. .*One Day at a Time!*

IDEAS/POINTS TO PONDER:

- Identify that thing(s) you are ashamed of...

- Fill in the blank: God has forgiven _____ and is going to use my mistake(s) to change someone's life.

- Who is in your life that reminds you of you?

- What can you do to help them?

_____
_____
_____
_____
_____
_____
_____
_____
_____
_____
_____
_____
_____
_____
_____
_____

DAY TWO

Proverbs 2:6 (NIV)

For the Lord gives wisdom; from His mouth come knowledge and understanding.

He Still Speaks

In this chapter Solomon outlines the rewards of wisdom. It is a list of benefits for the individuals that take time to search for wisdom like a hidden treasure. Moments like this... You picked up this book to figure out how to improve your character and how to connect with God on a deeper level.

The beauty of this text is that He wants to speak... to you. "Out of His mouth come..." GOD WANTS TO SPEAK TO YOU!!! Let that sink in for a moment! The Creator of the Universe has a desire to connect with you on an intimate level. You may say, "I've never heard God speak to me." "I don't know if I'm good enough to hear God." "What if I'm the exception?" Good news! I felt that way too, but I was crazy enough to believe that He speaks and guess what...He does.

But how do I know it is really God's voice? Good question! When I was trying to figure out God's voice, I used the following process.

- Is what I'm asked to do right?
- Do I want to do it? If the answer is no, then it's probably God! – I usually don't want to do what He says do!
- Will it help someone else?
- Is it something that I might need a power that is greater than myself to do?

At the end of the day, you may or may not agree to my list, or have your own, but know He still speaks. You hold in front of you an idea that He shared with me to help you. What if God has a Word for you today that can help someone as well? Spend the day being intentional about hearing Him, and make sure you listen, each day... *One Day at a Time!*

Ideas/Points to Ponder:

- How do you know that God is speaking?

- What is God saying (or been trying to say) to you today?

- Take a moment to write down what He is sharing with you.

_____
_____
_____
_____
_____
_____
_____
_____
_____
_____
_____
_____
_____
_____
_____
_____

DAY THREE

꙳

Proverbs 3:3 (KJV)

Let not mercy and truth forsake you: bind them about your neck; write them upon the table of your heart.

꙳

Embrace The Pain!

I've never had a tattoo, but I've heard that the pain can be excruciating, especially the ones that are on sensitive areas of the body... like the neck. Solomon is not advocating tattoos, but something that is just as long-lasting yet possibly even more painful! He challenges us to engrave mercy and truth on other sensitive areas – our hearts and minds.

Mercy can simply be understood as goodness or kindness extended to someone who does not deserve it. That means, extending mercy to someone when their actions do not warrant our favor. Truth, on the other hand, implies the idea of firmness or faithfulness. While this sounds simple, there are moments in the day, where a little lie could keep you out of trouble – or so it may seem.

Is this easy? Nope. Does applying mercy and telling the truth mean that we will seem out of step with society? Definitely. Is it possible you could be taken advantage of or viewed as weak? Absolutely... at least in the eyes of men. But heaven's approval promises a far greater reward than momentary happiness and temporary gain.

I challenge you to give someone a pass today. Let someone off the hook for something that you and the other person know deserves punishment. I dare you to tell the truth even if it may cause you personal pain, or when a tiny white lie could momentarily advance your cause. While it may not be easy, embrace the pain, as you take it... *One Day at a Time!*

Ideas/Points to Ponder:

- Has anyone ever extended mercy to you?
- Why do you think you remembered that event?
- Practice extending mercy to someone today and briefly describe his or her reaction below.

_____
_____
_____
_____
_____
_____
_____
_____
_____
_____
_____
_____
_____
_____
_____
_____

DAY FOUR

Proverbs 4:4 (NKJV)

He also taught me, and said to me: "Let your heart retain my words; Keep my commands and live.

Obedience = Life

One adage says, "A drowning man will grasp for a straw." Even though a rational person knows the inability of a straw's buoyancy to sustain their weight, conventional wisdom is thrown out the window when we are desperate. At times, we think we are so far away from the possibility of dying, that not only do we grasp for straws, we go deeper in the water believing we can get out any time we choose. Let me be clear today... *The Devil is like a roaring lion seeking whom he can devour (1 Peter 5:8).* As declared in Revelation 12, the enemy is out to make war with those who are living during the close of earth's history. The Devil is not interested in throwing you a party, nor does he want to become your best friend, so you can live happily ever after. His sole goal is to keep you out of the kingdom of God by destroying your life!

What is our defense? The Devil knows he only has this last ounce of time. So, how do we stand in the face of such a diabolic, conniving, wicked, deceitful, cunning, and relentless foe? Solomon simply says, "Keep my commands and live" Proverbs 7:2. Obedience to the Word of God is the only fortress, sole defense and offensive weapon that we have to combat the forces of darkness! Isaiah 1:18 says it best, "If you be willing and obedient, you will eat of the good of the land, but if you refuse and rebel, you will be devoured by the sword." If we want to live, we must stay in the Word and be obedient to our Lord! Yes, obedience = life and living begins as we obey. So, make time not only to read the word, but keep God's commands and live...*One Day at a Time!*

IDEAS/POINTS TO PONDER:

- Memorize the today's scripture (begin by writing it three times below).

- What is God telling you to do that you have a difficult time following?

- Make today the day you fully obey and briefly describe the journey below.

_____
_____
_____
_____
_____
_____
_____
_____
_____
_____
_____
_____
_____

DAY FIVE

֍

Proverbs 5:20 (NKJV)

For why should you my son, be enraptured by an immortal woman, and be embraced in the arms of a seductress?

֍

Stay Faithful

It is almost like the pot calling the kettle black. How in the world could Solomon think to pen something like this? I can hear one of his 700 wives or 300 concubines in the background asking, wondering, and complaining, about the lack of attention they were getting. I cannot fathom what Christmas or birthdays were like. With the number of wives he had, did they even have anniversary celebrations?

But in instructing his son, Solomon dedicates the entire chapter to being faithful to one woman. Maybe the life of trying to take care of over 500 women began to wear on him. Could it have been that in this chapter the wise sage was wishing for his younger days again. Yearning against the possibility beyond an impossible reality to retrace and retract his lust-filled youth. Oh, how he may have wished to embrace his high school sweetheart and watch her grow old in his arms rather than the estrogen filled three-ring circus, which is now his unfortunate reality.

"Why should my son be caught up in the arms of an immoral, ungodly, non-believing, two-timing, unsanctifed, woman? Solomon pleads for his son not to be involved with this type of woman...

When we give ourselves intimately and emotionally to another, it compromises our ability to think clearly. Most importantly, it can serve as a wedge or an adhesive in our relationship with God. Today, examine your relationships. But before that, examine yourself. If someone were to "hook up" with you, would you lead them to Christ, or would it be the beginning of a slippery slope towards the "hot place"? May today's verse be a reminder for some, and a wakeup call to others that if he/she does not love God, he or she can never truly love you. Until tomorrow, take it...*One Day at a Time!*

Ideas/Points to Ponder:

- What is the source of your seduction?
- What damage is that seduction causing?
- Change your life by running & praying every time you are tempted! It won't be easy, but your life depends on it!!!

DAY SIX

❧

Proverbs 6:6 (NKJV)

Go to the ant, you sluggard! Consider her ways and be wise...

❧

Find An Ant!

With all his laboratories, and scientists and host of other scholars at his disposal, Solomon, the wisest man that ever lived, could have chosen any number of resources to teach his son about wise stewardship. I can see him pensively writing these messages to his son. Trying to decide the best way to illustrate the danger of being lazy... I can see him pause at the sight of a moving piece of bread scurrying ever so quickly along the baseboard of the palace. Upon closer examination, the wise sage realizes the bread isn't moving itself, but there is an ant, half the size of the moving object, diligently following other ants to carry the new-found treasure back to its nest.

In contrast to the ant, Solomon calls his son a "sluggard." Picture, its slimy body slowly oozing along the sidewalk leaving a slimy trail of mucus in its wake. The "slime" that coats the slug's body, serves to protect it from other animals, but they go nowhere fast. Whether Solomon wanted his son to get himself in gear or simply wanted to make a point, we do not know. However, one thing is clear, Wisdom doesn't come simply by asking, it is obtained through hard work, study, and perseverance. In other words, "Wisdom works." One motivational speaker shared "Greatness is never on sale. Champions never bring coupons." In light of the contrast between the ant and the slug, wisdom is nestled in the work ethic and attention to detail and efficiency of the ant. Take time to learn the lessons from the ant... *One Day at a Time!*

Points to Ponder:

- Take a few minutes to go outside to study an ant.

- Describe the ant's activities. Was the ant's path clear or did it have to maneuver around obstacles to accomplish its task?

- Identify what is keeping you from being like the ant? What areas of your life can be addressed today for you to maximize your potential?

_____
_____
_____
_____
_____
_____
_____
_____
_____
_____
_____
_____
_____
_____

DAY SEVEN

❧

Proverbs 7:1 (NIV)
My son, keep my words, and lay up my
commandments with thee.

❧

Listen!

Solomon takes us to a place that is real, for some, too real. Solomon begins this chapter with a plea to his son, "MY son, keep my words, and lay up my commandments with thee."

Solomon, watching from his window, sees a young man; old enough to make decisions, yet too young and foolish to realize one bad decision can change the rest of his life. She saw him too. He couldn't have been going anywhere special, nor did he have a major purpose on his mind. She saw him, kissed him and he just knew she was the one! Unfortunately, she was just playing him, and he found out that this "chance encounter" was not of God.

The plea before the old sage tells the story is for his son to listen to him. Many, young and old, are in trouble now because they did not listen to wise counsel. You may think they are dumb, they don't make any sense, the things they do are outdated, their rules are antiquated, the things they ask of you are for people younger than you, you may even think that you know more than they do. This text warns that one day it may cost you your life. "Keep my words" is more than a casual, "Hear what I am saying to you". The Message Bible says, "Do what I tell you, treasure my careful instructions." It reminds me of the admonition God gave to his servant Joshua after the death of Moses. The Bible records these words, *"Ponder and meditate on it day and night, making sure you practice everything written in it. Then you'll get where you're going; then you'll succeed (Joshua 1:8,MSG).* Take time to not only hear but also to listen to Godly counsel *One Day at a Time!*

Ideas/Points to Ponder:

- Read Proverbs 7. Are you the young man or the seductress?

- How many people do you know have found themselves hurt in similar situations?

- Who do you have to remove from your life to keep you from falling into the same scenario?

_____
_____
_____
_____
_____
_____
_____
_____
_____
_____
_____
_____
_____
_____

DAY EIGHT

ಶಿ

Proverbs 8:8 (NKJV)

All the words of my mouth are with righteousness;

Nothing crooked or perverse is in them.

ಶಿ

Use Only Godly Words!

How confident must we be to declare that *all* our words are with righteousness? Just think of the things you said this morning that might disqualify you from this testimony. At this very moment, accept this task by inviting the Holy Spirit to raise your level of communication. He alone can retrain our brains to compute and distribute only "wise words."

Will it be challenging? Absolutely, and without question! Do you or I have the ability to make the change overnight, doing it day-by-day or even moment-by-moment? No, but that doesn't stop us from putting this lesson into practice. If we truly want to grow, we must expect struggle!

It means you might have teeth marks on your tongue because you are biting down so hard trying to keep unrighteous words from coming out, but realize that the experience is normal...and essential! Living God's Word is going to challenge, stretch, prune, and trim our character in such a way that when it is all said and done, we will be better people and have a deeper relationship with Christ and with others.

Yes, it's hard work, no doubt about it! But no one wakes up and says, "Today, I've got my tongue under control and I'm not going to make any mistakes!" Yeah, right! Only through the power of Christ can that happen!

Today, I challenge you to speak words that are of God! Words that will edify, uplift, encourage and inspire. In all of your conversations, be positive and include no mischief, gossip, or backbiting, knowing that only through Christ change will happen...*One Day at a Time!*

Ideas/Points to Ponder:

- Why is it so difficult to speak "righteous words" throughout the day?

- What must you do to change that pattern?

- How can God be glorified by your words today?

DAY NINE

❧

Proverbs 9:10 (NIV)

The fear of the Lord is the beginning of wisdom,
and the knowledge of the Holy One is
understanding.

❧

Fear The Lord?

For a long time, I grappled with this text. I was perplexed by the admonition in this passage. What does it mean to fear the Lord? Do I walk around hunched over, pensively taking each step in fear that a herculean figure will pop out of the clouds and annihilate me because I did something stupid? Does it mean that I must sit in the back of the church until my life reflects Christ inching my way to the front, pew by pew, after spending years praying and fasting, memorizing the New Testament? You may have thought, "I'm already scared, and I don't need any more encouragement to "Fear the Lord!"

I remember, as I was planning for the previous entry, I came across this same phrase. It came from Proverbs 8:13 which says, "The fear of the Lord is to hate evil...." It didn't mean much when I read it because honestly, I was afraid already. I've come to the realization that fearing the Lord is simply hating the things He hates. It is shunning the things He shuns, avoiding the things that He doesn't condone. Fearing God is NOT about being afraid of Him, but simply, BECOMING LIKE HIM in thought and action! Wisdom begins when we like what God likes and run from things He does not like – EVIL! Yes, evil comes in all shapes and sizes, but most importantly, it germinates from our ideas! Before you pat yourself on the back or check off a list of things you don't do, remember, evil starts in the mind! Once it is established in your brain, evil translates into your actions. Today, let's ask God to help us fear Him, by loving the things He loves and running from the things He hates. If we truly want to be wise today, begin by getting to know the Lord through His word. With His power, we will think and act like Him as we walk together, taking it...*One Day at a Time!*

Ideas/Points to Ponder:

- What was your understanding of "Fear the Lord?"

- What can you do today to begin your journey with Christ?

_____
_____
_____
_____
_____
_____
_____
_____
_____
_____
_____
_____
_____
_____
_____
_____

DAY TEN

̀ℴ

Proverbs 10:4 (NIV)

Lazy hands make for poverty, but diligent hands bring wealth.

̀ℴ

Work Hard!

This promise is just as true as the Second Coming and just as comforting as Psalms 23. God promised, as stated in Proverbs 10:4, when you work hard, you will become rich. There is a reward for hard work! One of my favorite motivational speakers, Eric Thomas puts it this way, "Without struggle, there is no progress."

If you want to realize your dreams, be true to the calling that God gave you! For your dreams to become a reality, whether you want to advance in business, science, or any enterprise, it's essential that you work...and work HARD!

The book of Proverbs asserts that hard work pays off! There will be times when it may not appear that you are making strides or that the results are not coming fast enough. Even worse, you or a loved one may suggest that your labor is, in effect, just a waste of time! Remember, the Bible does not say that the road will be easy, or that you will immediately reap a large harvest from your work. Matter of fact, if you were to plant an orange, it would not sprout large juicy oranges a week after being placed in the ground. Consequently, we must acknowledge the principles of growth as we make preparation in our life.

Ecclesiastes 9:10 states, *"Whatever your hands find to do, do it with all your might.[1]"* Accept this assignment and work hard! It doesn't matter what it is—a difficult class, practicing an instrument, learning a new skill, or working at your present job. Whatever it is ---STAY FOCUSED and WORK HARD! Keep plugging away! Keep showing up! Put your best in every task and you will live the promise

---

[1]Ecclesiastes 9:10; Colossians 3:23

found in today's Proverb *"...diligent hands bring wealth"...One Day at a Time!*

Ideas/Points to Ponder:

- Do you really want to achieve your goal, or do you just want to talk about it?

- What have you been putting off, that you know you would benefit from, if you continued to work at it?

_____
_____
_____
_____
_____
_____
_____
_____
_____
_____
_____
_____
_____
_____
_____
_____
_____

DAY ELEVEN

❧

Proverbs 11:22 (NKJV)
As a ring of gold in a swine's snout, so is a lovely woman who lacks discretion.

❧

Precious Things For Precious People

Why a pig? Why not a lizard, a cow or a chicken? Why a swine over a kangaroo, an opossum, or a ladybug? Pigs were detestable animals. The Israelites were not to touch or come in contact with anything that was related to swine. In this passage, Solomon is not only saying that something of value should not be given to something so detestable, but he likens the waste of the gold to a lovely woman who lacks discretion or wise judgment.

You may have seen her. She was the cutest girl in the school. Every guy wanted to date her, every girl wanted to be her. She was full of promise, voted to be most popular, the most likely to succeed. Ten years later, at the reunion, she arrives, and it looks like life has ravished her beauty and hard times have robbed her of her youthful vitality. After a few questions, it is evident that associating with the wrong crowd and missing an opportunity to get out of the "game" she was too far in to get out. No longer destined for greatness, now simply struggling to survive.

But your life doesn't have to turn out or remain like this. The Bible writer says this is the lot of a lady (or man) that lacks discretion. Today we are going to learn from our past mistakes. Not only learn from them but also apply the Divine mandate to make wise decisions.

You may have made mistakes in your past. Possibly that is the reason you are finally picking up this book and have gotten this far. Today, the verse encourages us to save our valuables (in every sense of the word) for special people. ***No longer are we going to share precious things with temporary people.*** Start today and take it...*One Day at a Time!*

Ideas/Points to Ponder:

- What precious thing(s) have you shared with people that don't deserve them?

- Jot down a few benefits of discretion.

DAY TWELVE

Proverbs 12:15 (NKJV)
The way of a fool is right in his own eyes; but he that heeds counsel is wise.

You're Not That Smart!

If we look at our lives, we shutter at some of the decisions we made that came without listening to wise counsel. I reflected on one of my previous experiences with a young lady friend that I knew was an angel sent from heaven. I knew she was special; I was excited, elated, exuberant and ecstatic every time I saw her. But my bubble of emotions was busted when my family, all at different times, said she was not the one. What heartache, headache and at times "tummy aches" when I came to the harsh reality that they were right, and I was wrong. I went all in, gave it all I had, examined the friendship with every moral fiber I had in my little mind at the time. Only to find out that although she was a great young lady, she just wasn't the one for me. They were correct, and I had to admit that I was wrong. The situation could have been worse had I not listened to my family, that loved me, that was looking out for my best interest.

Your situation may not be a relationship, it could be a business venture, choosing a major, or where you should work for your summer job. Wisdom is not found in being independent, it is found in depending on and trusting in the wisdom of people God has placed in your life. We can't go back and undo all of our decisions, but we can begin today surrounding ourselves with godly people and listening to their advice. This means you will have to humble yourself and realize that you cannot answer every question and have every answer. Trust God and the people He's put in your life to help you...*One Day at a Time!*

IDEAS/POINTS TO PONDER:

- Why do you think it is difficult to listen to the advice of Godly people?

- Reflect on a few of the poor decisions you've made in your life? How could it have been better had you listened to someone with more knowledge in those areas?

DAY THIRTEEN

☙

Proverbs 13:24 (NKJV)
He who spares his rod hates his son, But he who loves him disciplines him promptly.

☙

Discipline Won't Kill You!

The more I read Proverbs, the more I see that it was written for parents. Not only for parents but parents with boys. One day, my wife and I overheard our boys saying that we were "mean" because we did not allow them to do an activity they wanted to do. Please understand that one was in trouble for something that was done previously in the day and he was not disciplined for it in the "traditional way."

The kids said we were "mean" because we did not allow them to do what they want when they want to do it. Mean was not waiting for 90 minutes in the hot sun for them to finish with soccer practice. Mean is not allowing them to have pizza money each week. Mean is not allowing them to go to friends' houses, or hang out late, or go outside to play with bikes, or to have a bike in the first place. No, we are not mean, we are simply committed to discipline.

I am a father; consequently, my children and I are not best friends. We are not buddies, we are not "cool", or "homeboys." Consequently, I will do some things that my boys do not like. I will make decisions that they will not understand. I will take actions that they will not always agree with. That is what parenting is - making decisions for the greater good, rather than trying to appease my children.

Today, the challenge is to trust God when He treats us like I treat my sons! The Bible says that the lack of discipline is the equivalent of leaving your kid on the street without food or shelter; equal to abuse or just plain old hatred. Love says, "I won't let you do what you want because I want something better for you." When you are disciplined, know that you are loved...*One Day at a Time!*

IDEAS/POINTS TO PONDER:

- What is the worst part of the discipline process?

- How do you respond to discipline from your parents?

- How do you react when you are disciplined by God?

_____
_____
_____
_____
_____
_____
_____
_____
_____
_____
_____
_____
_____
_____

DAY FOURTEEN

❧

Proverbs 14:5 (NKJV)

A faithful witness does not lie, but a false witness will utter lies.

❧

Tell The Truth

Today's proverb is pretty straightforward. It challenges us to tell the truth. Here the old sage takes out two crayons and draws a picture on our imagination of two people on a jury stand reporting the facts as they saw them. On one hand, you have individual A who tells the story without embellishing any of the details. Individual B, however, skews the facts, changes names and tells a host of other untruths to sway the judge and the jury. Sometimes the liar, the cheater, the untruth teller sways the jury in his favor, but the Christian operates under a different set of rules. To be truly wise, to be like Christ, we are compelled to tell the truth regardless of how good a lie may sound.

Today, we must tell the truth. Not only in situations that favor us or in circumstances where we look good, but also when we are in situations that may reveal we were in error, we must tell the truth. Because you are reading this, God will work your day out where you will have to encounter the reality of this Proverb. There will be a litmus test that will reveal whether you stand for truth or buckle under the temptation to lie. You may have a tendency to tell a "white lie" in a pinch. "It isn't that bad," you say, "but the story sounds so much better with a little more imagination." Not today. Today, no lying lips, no fudging facts, no smearing specifics, and no diminishing details. If there is someone who claims to be a Christian and proclaims to follow THE FAITHFUL WITNESS[2], then we must strive to live the way He did. And today, with His help, you can.... as you take it...*One day at a Time!*

---

[2] Revelation 1:5

IDEAS/POINTS TO PONDER:

- What makes telling the truth so difficult?

- Is there a particular area where you find it more difficult to tell the truth than in others? Taxes, sports, at work, in relationships, etc.? Why?

DAY FIFTEEN

☙

Proverbs 15:1 (NKJV)

A soft answer turns away wrath, but a harsh word stirs up anger.

☙

Respond Kindly

After fighting with my older brother, it would always happen that my mother would catch me or stop me before I had a chance to respond or retaliate. Perhaps I was too slow, or he was so quick that I never got a chance to hit back. I would find ways, other, more hurtful ways to get back at him. Once cooler heads prevailed, or when she took out the belt, she would sit me down and say, "someone always has to get hit last to end a fight." Her words stung because I was always the one that got hit last! I'm not sure if my mom read this Proverb, but the principle takes her words to a different level. To end a quarrel, we have to do something completely opposite for it to truly cease.

This request is not natural. It is not ingrained in you (definitely wasn't in me!). It challenges our Christian experience because this isn't something we can pray about and walk away. Today, I have to face people who have done something wrong or are feeling (as the young people say) "some kinda way". You may look at this text and say, "I will pick another text for today," but face the uncomfortable reality that when wrath comes my way, I usually and preferably, respond in kind. Often times, my wrath is worse than the level that was initially displayed toward me.

Today we are practicing kind responses. It is challenging to embrace another person's pain and hurt. I am not telling you this would be easy, there isn't much in our Christian experience that is. Today the prayer is to ask God to give you the words to say, and the temperament to mean it! Remember, if it were easy, everyone would do it! Respond kindly today, as you take it...*One Day at a Time!*

Ideas/Points to Ponder:

- When was the last time you implemented this Proverb?

- Can you think of a time in your life that you wish you did?

- What was the outcome?

DAY SIXTEEN

֎

Proverbs 16:9 (NKJV)

A man's heart plans his way, but the Lord directs his steps.

֎

Let Him Lead!

I began the day thinking about what I had to do. What my plans for the day would be... trying to contemplate all the day's events and how they would get done in such a short time. As I was thinking about today, my mind began to go to the events of tomorrow, then that lead to how in the world I was going to make it later. I began to get overwhelmed because my mind was trying to grapple with the decisions of the week (which I felt were mostly bad) and how this text relates to my life today. By the end of the day, I was stressed!! I came to realize that I can plan my way, but God directs my steps.

What are your plans today? What are you grappling with that is causing you to stay up at night or keeping you from focusing on things at hand? Today, our focus is to allow God to do what His Word says He does.

There is a popular commercial that begins by showing a man with a white lab coat using a jackhammer in a construction site. The narrator says, "You wouldn't want your doctor doing your job so why try to do his?" I think that is fitting with this passage, know what your role is and where God's place is. We can make all the elaborate plans in the world, but ultimately it is God who directs our steps. Today's challenge is to relinquish your plans for the day. Not that you abandon your plans, but you view your plans as if they were on a dry erase board rather than tables of stone. Make your plans today but view them in the lens that God is possibly and probably going to change them...For His glory. Until next time, take it...*One Day at a Time!*

IDEAS/POINTS TO PONDER:

- What plans do you have that are difficult to give to God?

- Write down how your plans could change (for better or worse) if you allow God to plan your steps?

DAY SEVENTEEN

❧

Proverbs 17:1 (NIV)
Better a dry crust with peace and quiet than a house full of feasting, with strife.

❧

Stuff Or Satisfaction – What Is Stressing You?

It hit me like a ton of bricks! I was about to go to bed after finishing a statistics assignment and I wanted to read Proverbs chapter 17 because I got so busy today that I neglected to spend time in the Word. It may sound strange to some, but there are days where I get so busy doing things *for* God that I neglect to spend time *with* God.

I opened the chapter on my phone and the verse that I have read a number of times before made me get out of bed and begin typing. "It is better to have a piece of a scrap with peace than a full house with strife." My boys have been sleeping on pallets on the floor, there were six people in a two-bedroom condo, we had no space, our dressers were the suitcases we came here (Huntsville, AL) with when we moved three months ago. We had a few clothes that we came with from Pennsylvania, no real study space, but looking back on this journey... I have had peace. That is the greatest blessing... being able to move across the country without a place to live and still have peace.

Our thought for today is to stop trying to get more stuff. Pause on trying to purchase that purse, give up on the new golf clubs, the wisest man that ever lived admonishes us today that it is better to be in a shack, a rundown shanty, a space you do not want nor think you deserve, than have the world at your disposal and not have peace. Be content with the little you have and enjoy the peace that comes with it. If all you have is a morsel...chew slowly as you take it...*One Day at a Time!*

Ideas/Points to Ponder:

- Where does your mind wonder when you have time to daydream?

- What does peace look like in your current situation?

- Is there anything that you are complaining about that if you received could add extra stress?

DAY EIGHTEEN

༒

Proverbs 18:22 (NKJV)
He who finds a wife, finds a good thing, and obtains favor from the Lord.

༒

Favor!

It has been 14 years and 130 days (and counting!) that I have been married to the love of my life. We have seen some great days, and there have been sometimes that we wondered why in the world did I marry this person? But through it all, the Proverb holds true, I have obtained favor from the Lord. My life has been enriched, I have been humble (and humbled), I have learned patience, and developed a host of other virtues. Marriage shows you how selfish you are and reveals a glimpse of how much our Savior sacrificed for us.

The focus of the text is on finding a wife. In this context f nding a wife is equal to, or synonymous with, the favor of God! In the Hebrew language favor means God literally smiling on you and has goodwill toward you. What an awesome thought!

For those who may be reading this that are not married, but are planning to be, know that God is in the process of making you a blessing, a love and a pleasure in someone's life you may have not even met yet!

How does one even get to this level? Ephesians admonishes husbands to love their wives like Christ loved the church and gave Himself up for it.

I have a bit of homework for you today. For all those men that are married - do something for your wife today to let you know how blessed you are for her being in your life. For those who are still looking – begin planning on the best way to prepare yourself for your spouse. Observe your life and see how God has given you favor...as you take it...*One Day at a Time!*

IDEAS/POINTS TO PONDER:

- Is it possible that you have experienced God's favor and not realized it?

- What did you do that got your wife's attention when you first met her that you have stopped doing?

- What areas can you see God's favor in your life?

- For the singles – what area(s) do you need to shore up to be a blessing for your future spouse?

_____
_____
_____
_____
_____
_____
_____
_____
_____
_____
_____
_____
_____

DAY NINETEEN

❧

Proverbs 19:20 (NKJV)
Listen to counsel and receive instruction, that you may be wise in your latter days.

❧

Listen To Wise Counsel

The first thing we have to acknowledge is that we don't know everything!!! There is something someone is going to teach you today that will help you be successful later in life. It may be from someone you may not ordinarily look to for wisdom or rely on for council, but today God has a message for you.

Don't forget the things you learned yesterday. The things you learn today may not be for you to use immediately. I have a hard time trying to be patient with information I can't use right at that moment. Immediate gratification rarely works in a prosperous life, and unfortunately for the Christian, **God grooms us using crockpots rather than microwaves**. It may be a while before we get that "ah ha" moment I remember someone telling me that before.

Take time to listen, it may add a few years to your life! As we grow today, we are going to take it...*One Day at a Time!*

Ideas/Points to Ponder:

- What are a few potential pitfalls that come from not listening to counsel?

- What is it that you know now that you wish you had listened to before?

DAY TWENTY

❧

Proverbs 20:4 (NKJV)

The lazy man will not plow because of winter; he will beg during harvest and have nothing.

❧

Work!

You have to work! There is nothing else to say for the day. You may have heard of Pareto's 80/20 rule, where 20% of your time you do 80% of your meaningful work. How many of our problems are not actual problems but excuses? I've learned that there is always something that is going to try to distract you, throw you off, change your plans, but at the end of the day you have to push through and work.

Winter affects everyone everywhere! Winter is not only for working people, winter is not solely for people that have things to do... The lazy man in the text is not working because of winter that will *potentially* stop him. Not working in the winter cannot be an excuse that will keep us from doing something... especially if that thing will help not only you but everyone around you.

What are the "winter" excuses in your life? Solomon challenges us to face the "winters" in our lives today. The lazy man won't work because of inconvenience, and the reality of life. There are people that are reading this book today, that will choose to skip this verse because it forces you to do something hard, something challenging. There are too many people that don't have what they would like or need because they have to face what successful people do every day – overcome the excuses. Today is the day you realize you are normal. You are not special because you have challenges, issues, difficulties, or problems. The reality of this text is that everyone has to face their excuses, but only the successful master them.

I started running a few weeks ago. I was unsure how this journey was going to work out because I am not one to get out of bed early. Through the course of my newfound experience, I tried to run a little further each day. One day last week, I pushed myself to run the hills (I strategically avoided last week) and to my surprise, I was able to finish the route and I felt better than I did any other day. No hills, no strength.

Plow is the name of the game today. Plowing in the winter is difficult, the ground is hard, the wind is chafing your skin, but if you want to eat later, you have to work now. This Proverb isn't just for an agrarian society, it is a word to those that look at the difficulties in life and say, "I won't, I can't, I'm scared." Blisters may develop, your back may ache, the climate may be unforgiving, but at the end of the day, work now or starve later.

The theme for this journey is one day at a time... Today take the plow out of the shed and work the field. It may be homework, a project you have been putting off, a book you have been saying you were going to write, whatever your "winter is" face it and see how God will reward your faithfulness. Go to Work!

Ideas/Points to Ponder:

- Based on this text, is there something you could have more of if you worked a little harder?

- Write down the specific "winters" in your life. Br efly describe the potential benefits in your life once you have conquered them.

DAY TWENTY-ONE

❧

Proverbs 21:13 (NKJV)

Whoever shuts his ears to the cry of the poor will also cry himself and not be heard.

❧

Help Somebody

An old song says, "If I can help somebody as I walk along. If I can cheer somebody with a word or song. If I can show somebody that they are traveling wrong. Then my living shall not be in vain." This verse jumped out at me today because today is a day to get outside of yourself. This isn't a self-help book that focuses solely on you and how to improve you and everything is centered on your desires. No, today's Proverbs challenges us to look beyond ourselves to help someone else. The cyclical nature of the proverb indicates that while it may not be you in need right now and during this season, you will one day need assistance for something. Therefore, when you have an opportunity to help someone and you do not, the universe is wired in such a way, that you will receive the same type of treatment that you gave to someone else. It is an outgrowth of the Golden Rule: do what you would like other people to do to and for you. It may not be you that directly benefits, it may be that someone helps your child or relative the same way you extended yourself to them.

This is also going beyond working with people that you like, or like you. Today, God is going to bring some people your way that need your help and there may not be anything they can do to return the favor. You may not feel like you are able to do it, may not think you have the resources, but try to place yourself in their shoes and fight for them like it is your problem, your issue, your need. Watch how God turns things around for you...*One Day at a Time!*

IDEAS/POINTS TO PONDER:

- Why do you think Solomon admonishes us not to walk away from assisting others?

- Describe how you would feel if, or when, someone helped you in your time of need.

- How can one benefit from helping people in need?

DAY TWENTY-TWO

❧

Proverbs 22:1 (NKJV)
A good name is to be chosen rather than great riches, loving favor rather than silver and gold.

❧

Focus On What Matters

Why would Solomon say a good name is better than riches? At the end of the day what really matters?

This verse is countercultural. The verse goes against the grain. This verse is strange. So strange that many reading this text, may want to skip to another verse for the day.

The Bible naturally takes a position that is not only countercultural but opposite of our natural desire. Some will say, "I'll take a bad name as long as I have money." Unfortunately, money is fleeting and the closer one gets to it, the further it moves out of your grasp. It is like putting your hand in a bucket of water and attempting to pull out enough water to make a hole. Your hand will pull out water, but never enough to make a hole. As a matter of fact, in a few seconds, your hand will be dry as if it never went into the water in the first place.

Notice the adjective "good" before name. Everyone has a name. You may not like your name, some have even gone to great lengths to change their name. While it isn't easy to change ones' name, it is in your power to change the adjective before your name. You choose the adjective by the decisions you make, by the people you choose to associate with, and the habits you form... all *One Day at a Time*. Today take time to examine your habits. Slow down enough to review who is in your favorites list in your phone. Use today to adjust the adjective in front of your name. If it is bad, begin today to turn it around. If you think it is good, what is keeping you from making it great? Today focus on what matters...and watch how God rewards your desire to trust Him...*One Day at a Time!*

IDEAS/POINTS TO PONDER:

- Do you prefer a good name or riches?

- How do your actions line up with the answer to the previous question?

- Briefly describe how a good name can surpass wealth and riches?

_____
_____
_____
_____
_____
_____
_____
_____
_____
_____
_____
_____
_____
_____
_____
_____

DAY TWENTY-THREE

ಈ

Proverbs 23:5 (NKJV)

Will you set your eyes on that which is not? For riches certainly make themselves wings, they fly away like an eagle toward heaven.

ಈ

The Chase

Once a week my family will take a walk around our neighborhood. There is a semi-wooded area along our path and geese are often found there searching through the grass for food (or whatever else geese look for in the grass!). When we get close to this area, our dog (a tiny Shi Tzu/mix) charges at the geese, two times bigger than she is, and without fail, they always fly away long before she gets anywhere close. She will run with all her might, come back to us huffing and out of breath... and she never catches even a feather of even the smallest bird of the flock.

We are often like the little dog chasing the geese when it comes to attaining wealth. We charge in its direction with all our might, only to get disappointed when it is gone just as soon as we get close. But there is something more important than money...We are on this earth to improve the lives of others. Our gifts and abilities to obtain financial resources should be used to help someone who does not have that same opportunity. In doing so, we mirror the character of our Creator, who is constantly giving to provide for our needs.

Our text challenges us to focus our attention on Christ's words in Matthew 6:19-20, *"Don't store up treasures here on earth where they can erode away or may be stolen. Store them in heaven where they will never lose their value and are safe from thieves."* Today, as you search for meaning and purpose, take inventory of how you are spending your time in an effort to get "rich". What have you been focusing your attention and energies on? Is it something that you can take with you to the kingdom or assist someone else to get there?

Take time to adjust your focus. Step back and assess whom you can help with your quest for financial gain. One of my favorite motivational speakers once remarked that "the more we are willing to give to others, that are not connected to us, the greater our reward will be." Who can you set your sights on today? Who is in your sphere of influence that will be blessed because of the financial blessing you receive? Start today to shift your gaze from getting, to giving, and watch how the Creator begins to bless...*One Day at a Time!*

IDEAS/POINTS TO PONDER:

- What has been your experience with the acquisition of wealth?

- If you had more money, what would you do with it? Honestly?

- How have you seen this Proverb play out in your life?

_____
_____
_____
_____
_____
_____
_____
_____
_____
_____
_____
_____
_____
_____

DAY TWENTY-FOUR

❧

Proverbs 24:10 (NKJV)

If you faint in the day of adversity, your strength is small.

❧

Man Up!

Life is going to happen. Life is going to happen. Life is going to happen. Life is...*(I think you get my point!)* Today's text is a wakeup call that life can be cruel, arduous, demanding, and exacting. Unfortunately for us, we don't have a choice to take a day off or go on a "life vacation". Solomon doesn't excuse or discount the sad and harsh realities of life – it isn't easy. He doesn't preface this statement with "For the non-Christian" or "for the unchurched". The day of adversity, the day of trial, the day of "I want to give up and throw in the towel"...those days come for the sinner and the saint. Solomon declares that our rough moments are considered a litmus test of our spiritual and mental fortitude.

Notice it is not a condemnation if one's strength is small, it is a matter of fact statement, that identifies and sheds light on the reality that we have to go back to the weight room of life and continue to prepare for challenges that come our way.

What is your current situation saying about your present level of spiritual strength? Are you trusting in God for strength or have you succumbed to the solution-less simplicity of a secular society? Are you preparing for adversity in the time of peace? It is easy to let one's guards down spiritually, when everything is going well. Bills are paid, credit is available, the family is getting along, grades are up, and teachers are not losing their minds... In times of peace, we tend to slack off of worship, trade the Bible for the television remote or other exercises that do not strengthen us spiritually.

No matter what position you find yourself in, adversity or peace, begin committing to memory texts that will sustain you through some of life's most difficult moments as you take it...*One Day at a Time!*

IDEAS/POINTS TO PONDER:

- Think about moments of fear in your life. What Bible text popped into your head during that experience?

- Begin memorizing Psalm 27. What does the author say about God's power and presence in difficulty?

DAY TWENTY-FIVE

❧

Proverbs 25:16 (NKJV)
Have you found honey? Eat only as much as you need, lest you be filled with it and vomit.

❧

Enough Is Enough

There is nothing better than having your favorite snack in your hands and you are in a special place where you don't have to share with your kids, friends or spouse. My kryptonite, is that bag of Cheetos that calls my name in the gas station. Not the small bag, the kind that says the serving size is for 3 or 4, (but I know that is a mistake). Within a few secret minutes of chomping away, the bag is just about gone, artificial cheese embedded in the ridges of my fingertips, it tasted so good, but my stomach hurts so bad. The joy of eating my favorite snack is whisked away by a churning stomach and a throbbing headache. Too much of a good thing can be a bad thing.

Today's Proverb reminds me of a television show that chronicled the stories of persons that kept way too much stuff. They are called "hoarders." These persons are so attached to what initially were good things, pets, cars, clothes, food, even tools, but over time the things consumed them to the point of injury or physical harm. Solomon cautions us that having everything we like all the time hurts more than it helps.

The point is very straightforward. Don't take too much of a good thing or it will cease to become a good thing. What you thought would be great will be spoiled by your inability to pace yourself or push away from that which was once so wonderful.

Today as you are intentional about character development, you have to learn to be content with what you have. Secondly, the challenge is to take what you need…and the prayer today is, God help me to see what is enough. Our "honey" can be food, sports, a television series, an Internet site, or relationships…what is your "*it*"? Identify it and pray that God will help you get to the point where you are content with just enough as you take it… *One Day at a Time!*

IDEAS/POINTS TO PONDER:

- What is your "thing" that you enjoy a little too much?

- What safeguards can you establish to help you to have more self-control?

- Describe the benefits of being content with just enough?

DAY TWENTY-SIX

❧

Proverbs 26:11 (NKJV)
As a dog returns to his own vomit, so a fool repeats his folly.

❧

Learn From Your Mistakes

I have to be straightforward today because Solomon takes this wisdom thing to another level. As a visual person with a relatively weak stomach, I can't think on this verse too long. It may have come from a stomach virus, or after eating something that we didn't know was spoiled or a virus that has infected our body, but for whatever reason, our stomachs began to bubble and up comes our lunch. The stench is horrendous; there are chunks of un-chewed food particles mingled with whatever gastric acids that were flowing in our stomach...*I'm getting sick even writing this*. Dogs, Solomon says, return to that disgusting place, because what repels humans is what dog experts say is a delicacy for the canine. There is an appetizing quality to the vomit that brings the dog back.

Before we come down too hard on our four-legged friends, there may be a tiny bit of fool in you too. You have returned to the scene of your stupid decisions that others have said was dumb, ignorant and completely foolish. Not only did you return, but you did it again! It's the struggle Paul references where "the things that I don't want to do, those are the things I do (Romans 7:15). The only way out of the conundrum is trusting in Christ and those wise persons He has put in our lives to support and encourage us.

The lesson from today's Proverb is to learn from your mistakes! The problem in the text is not throwing up... we have all done that, but the issue is returning to it. We all make mistakes, but today, take time to learn from them. Take ownership of your actions. God has given us the ability to choose. Today you can flee from the messes in your life and start a new chapter in your decision-making process. You don't have to be perfect, but you have to put yourself in a position to be perfected...*One Day at a Time!*

IDEAS/POINTS TO PONDER:

- What area in your life do you find yourself repeatedly making the same mistake?

- Write down a few of the circumstances that surround that bad decision?

- Identify three things you can do to put yourself in a better position to succeed next time you are in a similar situation.

_____
_____
_____
_____
_____
_____
_____
_____
_____
_____
_____
_____
_____
_____
_____

DAY TWENTY-SEVEN

❧

Proverbs 27:1 (NKJV)
Don't boast about tomorrow, for you do not know what a day may bring forth.

❧

No Boasting!

You know what it's like to be afraid of the unknown, to fear the future, to be concerned about coming calamities. How often do you find yourself burdened by bungled blessings or plagued by sleeplessness because of worry over an unseen event? Whether those fears are caused by real or imagined threats, our text for the day takes us in another direction.

Our text cautions us not to be overzealous about tomorrow. Jesus tells a story of a man who had huge amounts of grain. He had so much that he told his servants to build bigger barns because his current warehouses couldn't contain his massive quantities. Yet, Jesus says what the man didn't know, was that day was his last on earth!

Now I'm not sharing that story to add to your fear or make you paranoid that you may die in your sleep tonight, but rather to caution you not to look for security down here. Not too long ago, a shooter walked into an elementary school and shot and killed innocent children. The truth is, no place is safe in this world! And the Bible tells us that it will only get worse. So, you may say, all the more reason to have fear! No, my friend, because the blessing is that we serve a God who knows the end from the beginning. Even when He allows negative things to happen in our lives, He works all things out for our good, and His glory!

So, as we think about today and plan for tomorrow, we should consider the assurance that heaven is promised for God's children, but this world is not it. No matter what happens on this earth, this earth is not the end. Our security comes from the promise that God is ultimately in control. Nothing takes Him by surprise, so we must put our trust in Him and lay claim to that peace that is consistent, even in the midst of uncertainties.

Neither planning nor worrying will bring us security. In fact, be careful of how you plan for tomorrow, because it will come with disappointments; yet, as we take it...*One Day at a Time*, we can be secure knowing that God holds tomorrow in His unchanging hand.

Ideas/Points to Ponder:

- Why is it sometimes easier to fret and worry than it is to trust God?

- Why would Solomon admonish us to focus on today and not expend so much of our energies on the future?

DAY TWENTY-EIGHT

꙳

Proverbs 28:1 (NKJV)

The wicked flee when no one pursues, But the righteous are bold as a lion.

꙳

Be Bold!

Growing up my brothers and I would play pranks on each other. Sometimes we would hide in closets or under the bed. We would jump out at the most unsuspecting time to scare each other. There were times when, after playing the game for a while, we would be afraid of a shadow, thinking it was a brother trying to get us. We were afraid to open closet doors, even when we could see each other because of the fear of a practical joke or the danger that someone was lurking on the other side.

People who do wrong are a lot like we were, scared to face things around corners because of what happened in the past. For the Christian, life should not be a place to hide. Today the Word encourages us to be bold. Understand that there is no one or nothing that can stand in the way of a righteous person that is moving in the power of God. So, go ahead! Try something new, speak out and speak up for what is right. Take an opportunity that you may not have thought possible yesterday. Why? There is something about stepping out of the comforts of casual and into the uniqueness of the unknown.

Today walk with your shoulders up, and your chest out. Face life courageously. The Psalmist pens in Psalms 46, that amid fleeing mountains and the earth opening up and closing, fear is not the vocabulary or the actions of a righteous person. The reason is found in Psalms 46:10, peace comes, not because there is anything special about us, but because we know that He is God. Remember that God is in control and He is controlling the universe for your benefit and His glory. Move out in boldness today as you take it... *One Day at a Time!*

IDEAS/POINTS TO PONDER:

- Name one God-given gift that you hesitate to use because of fear.

- What step can you take today to begin to face your fear(s)?

- What would you do if you weren't afraid?

DAY TWENTY-NINE

❧

Proverbs 29:9 (NKJV)
If a wise man contends with a foolish man,
whether the fool rages or laughs, there is no peace.

❧

Walk Away

Have you ever walked away from a long discussion, passionate about the point you are trying to make and yet the other person is looking at you lost and confused? Today, Proverbs informs us that there are some people that just are not going to get what you are trying to do or understand what you are trying to say. You can shout it from the rooftops, you can jump up and down while on fire (please don't try this), or you can stand on your head while spinning, and some people will still not "Get it."

As we grow to be more like Christ today, we are going to focus on walking away. You may be wondering, "shouldn't we persevere", or "what will happen if the individual just doesn't grasp the concept?" Well, this doesn't mean that we don't try, or if you are anything like me, want to classify everyone *else* as a fool – but prayerfully acknowledge that others will get it. Working hard, yet not seeing any progress with someone, yet the light bulb isn't going off and like the text says, "there is no peace." Walk away. Our time on earth is so short and because we are preparing for the Second Coming of Christ, we do not have time to waste our energy on foolishness or foolish people.

There is an old saying that goes something like this, "Know when to hold them, when to fold them, and when to walk away." Today, be careful how you spend your time. Don't stress yourself (or others) out by explaining and explaining and explaining to foolish people. Trust that God has multiple ways of reaching that person and today you may not be His chosen vessel!

And most importantly…make sure you are not that foolish person! Until tomorrow, take it…*One Day at a Time!*

IDEAS/POINTS TO PONDER:

- Be practical – what does it look like to "walk away"?

- How can you walk away and still remain respectful?

DAY THIRTY

❧

Proverbs 30:5 (NKJV)
Every word of God is pure: He is a shield to those who put their trust in Him.

❧

Trust God

I've never been shot before, but the movies make it look really painful! I have a few soldier friends that wear special body armor – similar to bulletproof vests – that repels bullets from puncturing their internal organs. The vests do not keep the solider from getting hit, but it does protect from the lethal impact of the bullet. I can imagine in Solomon's day; the shield served a similar purpose. The swords would be swung, or arrows sent screeching through the sky, but the soldier would be protected from the malicious intent of the enemy's weapons.

We have a promise that God's Word is similar to the bulletproof vest. Solomon says "He [God] is a shield to those who put their trust in Him." Life as we know it will have a number of "blows" that are designed to take us out, but God's Word serves as a defense, a lifesaving defense, that will prepare us for this life and the life to come. The real question is "Do we trust it"?

Today we are going to focus on trusting God's Word...**even when it may not make sense**. God knows our innermost thoughts. He longs to keep us from evil. He yearns to protect us from the consequences of bad choices. He truly desires to be our shield and He will...if we would simply trust Him.

Take time to memorize Psalm 46:1. Write it on an index card or use it as a screensaver on your phone or tablet. Whatever or however you deem it best to internalize this text. At the end of the day, identify how you have seen God be a source of protection for you...*One Day at a Time!*

Ideas/Points to Ponder:

- Why is it so hard to go to God first for help?

- Name the people and things you go to first for help.

- List practical ways to practice going to God first.

_____
_____
_____
_____
_____
_____
_____
_____
_____
_____
_____
_____
_____
_____
_____

DAY THIRTY-ONE

꙳

Proverbs 31:31 (NKJV)
Give her of the fruit of her hands; and let her own works praise her in the gates.

꙳

Affirm Your Mom

There is a temptation to write this only to the female readers. Proverbs 31 is well-known for its description of the perfect woman. Ministries are named after it, books have been written about it, but this text unearths gems that span beyond the reality of being a woman.

Solomon ends his wisdom literature with this sentence. There is a temptation to read into this text all the great things this woman has done. She accomplished great feats; she was a woman of virtue, hard work, and tenacity. She stuck to the task and the world marveled at her accomplishments.

The more I look at the text, the efforts this mother made are in danger of overshadowing the true meaning of this verse. The wise sage isn't so much highlighting the work done by this woman but emphasizing the response of the recipients of those efforts. Solomon cries out to those who have benefitted from nine months of labor, late night feedings, home cooked meals, intense prayers, sacrifices of untold proportions, he cries to the children of this woman, to publicly acknowledge what was done on their behalf.

On this the last entry of this experience, it is fitting that we end focusing on someone other than ourselves. Today's challenge is to publicly appreciate a maternal figure in your life. You may not have had the best mother or didn't grow up with a mother at all. It may have been a grandmother, an aunt, your best friend's mom, a dean or a big sister. You pick the person but let them know how much you appreciate them.

You may never know the whole story or all the sacrifices, but know, like the woman in this Proverb, you wouldn't be where you are without her. You are standing on the shoulders of greatness. Take time today to show your appreciation, today, every day and...*One Day at a Time!*

IDEAS/POINTS TO PONDER:

- Who is the maternal figure that has made the biggest impact on your life? Why?

- In what way have her sacrifices been appreciated?

- Briefly describe how you can share those gifts/sacrifices with the next generation?

_____
_____
_____
_____
_____
_____
_____
_____
_____
_____
_____
_____
_____
_____
_____

Conclusion

Each day of the month we read an entire chapter of Proverbs as indicated by the day's date. With each day, you got an opportunity to look over my shoulder into verses that impacted me. But that was last month. You have the tools, you have the tenacity to stay in the Word for an entire month, and most importantly, you have the Creator that will guide you into all truth.

The next phase of the journey is yours. You have the challenge to go back through the first chapter of Proverbs identifying the text that spoke to you, that challenged your spiritual growth, one that pushed you to make practical changes in your daily journey. You know change does not happen overnight, but little by little, *One Day at a Time*, God will unleash powerful changes in your life. Gradually, some days instantaneously, you will begin to identify just how practical the Word of God is.

Proverbs was written by the smartest man that ever lived and yet who also made some of the dumbest mistakes in history. Women separated him from his God. Pleasure led him from an intense connection with his family and his children. The nation of Israel was blessed through his reign, but the legacy of impropriety ravished God's people for generations. Somehow in spite of all of his misgivings and mess-ups, God still used him to aid you and I in a journey that will forever change our lives...*One Day at a Time!*

About the Author

Dr. Toussaint Williams has been an active member of the pastoral and teaching profession for the past 14 years. He spent countless hours working with high school and college students (as well as older Christians) that simply want to know how to apply God's Word in a practical way. Toussaint is an avid educator and enjoys using creative methods to teach spiritual lessons to audiences of all ages. Due to a number of experiences in a variety of locales, he and his wife have gained numerous insights about the Christian journey, marriage, and family health that they are delighted to share.

Dr. Toussaint Williams is a pastor, educator and a lifelong learner. He has a Ph.D. in Character Education, a Master of Divinity and recently completed an MBA in Finance. He is currently serving as an Associate Pastor, while also teaching courses in several disciplines at the university level. In addition to writing, Toussaint is passionate about his family and their well-being. He and his wife have two active sons, Eleazar and Uriah. They are committed to sharing their personal journey, through the lens of God's ideal as outlined in the Bible, in ways that will assist fellow Christians with the real-life highs and lows of following God. He has learned that life's journey brings uncertainties and calls for an unwavering faith – one that grows...*One Day at a Time.*

Email: Info@ToussaintWilliams.com

Website: www.ToussaintWilliams.com

Twitter: @DrToussaintWill

Instagram: @DrToussaintWill

www.ingramcontent.com/pod-product-compliance
Lightning Source LLC
Chambersburg PA
CBHW050618130526
44591CB00045B/2297